HOME SERIES
SPACES FOR LEISURE

BETA-PLUS

CONTENTS

P. 4-5
The swimming pool of a country home constructed by Vlassak-Verhulst and designed by Christel De Vos and Bjorn van Tornhaut (Sphere). The pool is surrounded by bluestone tiles and lined with a Bisazza glass mosaic. Rattan furniture by Cleybergh.

P. 6
The music room in a house designed by Costermans. The floor is made of reclaimed solid oak floorboards from France.

INTRODUCTION

Increasingly the home is becoming a refuge where you can escape the hectic pace of the world outside and forget the worries of day-to-day life.

Whatever the leisure activity – home cinema, reading, afternoon nap, swimming or other sports – increasing importance is being attached to the interior design and aesthetic qualities of rooms dedicated entirely to rest and relaxation.

The features in this publication showcase some exceptional leisure spaces, all of which have been designed to maximise the occupants' sense of wellbeing.

P. 8
Fitness room with granite floor and a view over the garden. A Stephanie Laporte design (The Office).

P. 10-11
Bushy shrubs ensure a harmonious transition between the formal garden, swimming pool and wooded area at the back of this country villa.

A JEWEL OF A COUNTRY GARDEN

This distinctive country house in beautiful natural surroundings, complete with pond, was created by the architect Bernard De Clerk. He designed the garden as an extension of the house. The swimming pool wall and the rows of flourishing box trees, yew trees and hawthorn bushes invite idle contemplation.

The Moris Group provided the majority of the plants and simplified the layout of the garden. The pond was extended so that it could be seen from the house and the plants were limited to indigenous species.

The large solitary box trees (around 20 years old) were supplied and planted by the Moris Group.

The layout of the garden was simplified in order to make the most of the natural surroundings.

P. 16-17
The outdoor swimming pool is surrounded by a yew tree hedge. To the left is a maple hedge.

AN INSPIRING GAMES ROOM

The spaces and proportions in this country home created by architect Stany Dietvors are perfectly balanced.

The connections between the different spaces have been ingeniously thought out, as is beautifully demonstrated by the recently refurbished recreational room and adjoining bedrooms.

The use of low storage units in this multi-purpose room – serving as a television room, games room, rest room and more – creates a Zen atmosphere and a sense of comfort and space.

P. 18-19
The furniture and cupboards were created by Borja Veciana. The cupboards serve as storage space for toys. The settee was tailor-made by Durlet.

P. 20-21
The recreation-cum-games room was designed by Brussels-based interior architect Nicolas Dervichian.

EPISCOPAL INSPIRATION

T he swimming pool and home cinema in this house designed for a family with three young children were created by architect Bernard De Clerk in a classic eighteenth century style inspired by an Episcopal residence from 1750.

The flow of light into the building, the creation of angles and the optimal positioning of the rooms were key considerations in the design of this home. All of the rooms, including the swimming pool and relaxation and leisure spaces are arranged around an interior courtyard so that sunlight penetrates the rooms for the majority of the day. The exception, of course, is the home cinema, which has a more intimate feel.

P. 22-23
The infinity pool. The floor is made of rust coloured lava stone.
The recreational space that adjoins the swimming pool provides access to the fitness room above the pool. A shower has been installed in a recess.

P. 24-25
Television room with wall-mounted projection screen. The mantelpiece is decorated entirely with stucco work.

POOL HOUSE OR PUB?

The pool house of this large country villa has been transformed by Sphere Interiors into a real-life pub with sombre colours, a padded leather bar, barrels, an ice machine and more.

No detail has been missed in creating this superb effect.

P. 28-29
The attic room has been furnished with a professional pool table and a carpet with underlay. The solid oak flooring in the children's games room has been stained wenge. The MDF cupboards are tailor-made.

SOOTHING MINIMALISM

The interior architecture firm 'Aksent has designed and created this swimming pool area for a large contemporary home in a style that oozes serenity and minimalism, without being stark and austere.

This exceptionally pure design, devoid of any disruptive and tiring visual stimuli, invites total relaxation.

P. 30-31
Warm wood and natural stone were chosen for this changing room.

P. 32-33
At the back, in the centre of the
photograph, is a Gong chaise
longue from Promemoria.

A MULTIMEDIA HAVEN

IN A 1935 APARTMENT

I n this 1935 "ocean liner" style apartment, interior architect Mario Bruyneel – working in close collaboration with the owner – has created a space that epitomises modern comfort and pays homage to the inter-war period.

The renovation maintains the simplicity of the architectural features. The choice of monochrome colours was inspired by the entrance hall décor and has enabled the architect to successfully incorporate original Art Deco and period features.

The apartment's multimedia room provides an excellent example of this stylistic approach.

P. 34-35
Comfort and contemporary touches are key features of this multimedia room created by Mario Bruyneel. The artwork is by Herman Braun Vega. The console unit houses all of the wireless data/audio/video equipment.

AN ORNAMENTAL GARDEN

WITH TIMELESS CHARM

T he garden of this exceptional home in an extensive former brasserie was created in 1994 as part of the meticulous restoration of the building over several years.

The photographs in this feature showcase the owners' talent. They have successfully combined their passion for beauty and timeless charm with their great joie de vivre and a discrete formal design. Every detail of their garden is the epitome of natural beauty.

The windows were salvaged from an old convent when it was converted into a school chapel. The large windows ensure a strong connection between the garden and the interior.

Tapestry cushions and a piece of antique Provencal quilted embroidery.

P. 38-39
Even though it was only created in 1994, the garden appears as if it has always been there and perfectly complements the atmosphere of the house.
In the background (photograph above) is a bronze sculpture entitled High Wind by the British artist Lynn Chadwick.

A POOL HOUSE

WITH ASIAN INFLUENCES

This pool house, designed by Nathalie Van Reeth, has been constructed using treated afrormosia to give it an Asian quality. The simplicity of the design means that the pool house perfectly complements its surroundings and the classic family house to which it belongs.

Despite the limited space, the pool house is large enough that you can take a peaceful shower or enjoy a relaxing sauna or Turkish bath.

Garden furniture by Royal Botania on the afrormosia terrace.

The interior furnishings are also made of afrormosia. The wooden wall panels have been whitewashed and left unvarnished.

The large bench has been covered using a waterproof fabric. Behind the wall are the sauna, Turkish bath and two open showers. The flat pebble flooring runs throughout the room.

The Turkish bath is decorated with zelliges in beige-brown shades.

The two open showers with flat pebble flooring and unvarnished whitewashed wood panels on the walls.

AN ORIENTAL, ZEN ATMOSPHERE

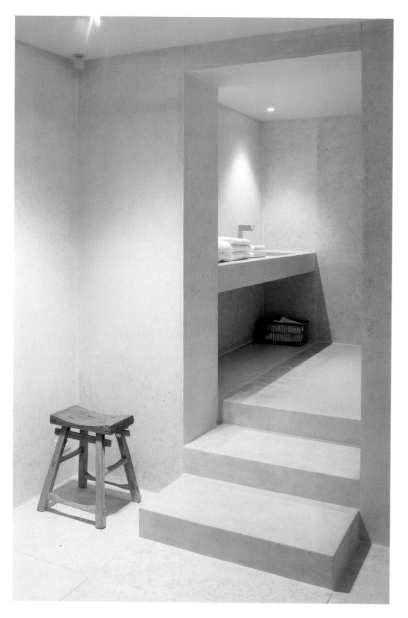

The entire basement (more than 100 m^2) of this large coastal villa has been transformed into a bathroom-cum-spa room comprising a Jacuzzi, bathtub, sauna, Turkish bath and hydro-jet shower.

The choice of materials and carefully selected lighting create a warm and soothing atmosphere. The design is minimalist, yet welcoming and cosy.

The beige-pink colour of the tadelakt plaster (a softer material than tiles) evokes an oriental spa and a place dedicated to well-being.

P. 46 to 49
Enormous tiles made from Massangis stone (a white stone quarried in France) were chosen for the floor. The walls also appear to be tiled in Massangis stone, but this is an illusion. In fact they have been painted using "faux marble" techniques that are so refined that it is impossible to distinguish the effect from the real natural stone. The simple, yet majestic, design is reinforced by a few exceptional well-chosen pieces: e.g. a nineteenth century distressed cabinet from Siena and a nineteenth century stool.

SIMPLE HARMONY

IN CLASSIC SURROUNDINGS

This swimming pool, designed by Christine von der Becke, integrates beautifully into this garden designed by Vincent Verlinden.

The pool house was designed by Nathalie Van Reeth.

P. 50-53
The terrace and swimming pool surround are made of bangkirai. The pool lining
is made of grey polyester.

P. 54-55
The old garages now house the open showers and changing room. The walls are decorated with black painted wood panels. Plumbing fittings by Boffi. The simple design complements the classic style of the house. The covered area, designed by Nathalie Van Reeth, is decorated with antique lamps and Moroccan cushions. The table top is made of reclaimed teak.

DREAM SWIMMING POOLS

These two dream swimming pools have one thing in common: both have been constructed using stone supplied by Van den Weghe, a specialist supplier of high-quality made-to-order natural stone.

P. 56-58
This exclusive indoor swimming pool
was designed by the architect Bernard
De Clerck.
For this design Van den Weghe used a
natural Pietra Piasentina stone with
flame-pattern finish, the surface of
which was smoothed out in places.

P. 59-61
This design by interior architect Lionel Jadot uses a combination of stippled Carrare marble and a natural lava stone from the Rome region.

AN OASIS OF PLENTY

This indoor swimming pool with roof terrace and drinks bar was designed by Olivier Campeert.

The long minimalist rectangular annex gives this classic house a modern touch and provides a refreshing bright space with an exceptional view over the garden.

The corridor between the house and swimming pool contains a shower, changing room and cellar. It also leads to a lift constructed to meet the owners' requirements.

The swimming pool has been carefully designed to maximise the flow of light and provide the owners with a place to display their hunting trophies.

P. 64-67
The walls consist of square panels against an illuminated background. The hanging fixtures are concealed behind each intersection enabling the owners to vary the arrangement of their trophies as they prefer.
A true oasis of plenty, the swimming pool comes complete with fully-equipped bar, the design of which mirrors the walls.
The floor is made of creamy yellow Massangis stone tiles and flagstones.

A TURKISH BATH MADE

OF PIETRA PIASENTINA

I n this bathroom with Turkish bath, designed by the architect Michel de Terschueren, the natural stone company Van den Weghe has used one of its specialities: north Italian Pietra Piasentina stone with flame-pattern finish is used throughout the design.

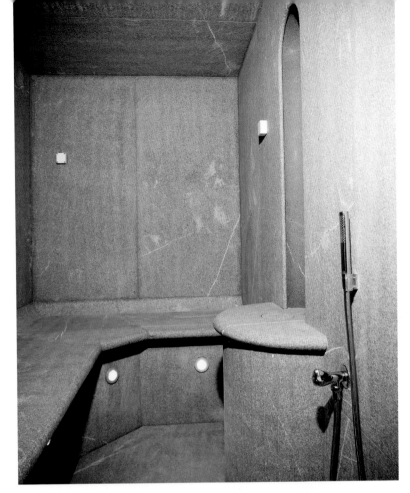

P. 70-71
The flame-pattern finish provides
an extremely practical anti-slip
function.

THE BENEFITS

OF A SAUNA AND TURKISH BATH

S auna House is a company that specialises in the production of saunas for private and commercial use.

Their exclusive and innovative models embody quality and aesthetics. Whether simple or luxurious, the designs can be adapted according to the client's wishes in order to complement their interior décor requirements.

Sauna House also produces a wide range of steam rooms. These can be supplied in different sizes, finishes and shapes in consultation with the client's interior architect.

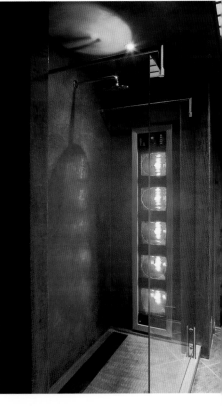

A HARMONY OF SPACE AND LIGHT

These leisure spaces form part of a large and luxurious contemporary home for a family with three children created by the architecture firm Crepain Binst. The interior design is by 'Aksent.

An important aspect of this project was to avoid creating a modern linear design that was cold and dreary. The designers therefore adopted a contemporary style that differs significantly from conventional designs. Starting points for the design were the concepts of past and future. Faithful to the philosophy of their favourite brand, Promemoria, the designers have created a space in which the connection to the past ensures an air of serenity, while the future aspect evokes a sense of suspense and expectation.

The bar is the most theatrical part of the house. Above the bar hangs a work by Panamarenko. The mobile stainless steel and leather stools were created by Karri Monni for Lapalma. The lighting was created by Bertjan Pot for Moooi.

Small pebble flooring was chosen for the children's bathroom. The interior panels of the cupboards are painted sky blue in order to evoke a real holiday atmosphere. There is one washbasin for each of the three children with mirrors that can be adjusted as they grow.
The pebble flooring continues into the shower. The walls are made of Portuguese sandstone.

P. 78-81

The cellar houses a leisure suite complete with Turkish bath, Jacuzzi, sauna, shower and swimming pool. The Turkish bath and Jacuzzi are decorated with a marble mosaic. The floor tiles are made of Combre Brune limestone. The teak wall panels give the space a touch of warmth. Loungers by Piet Boon. The entire swimming pool is decorated with black pebbles.

A WARM AND INTIMATE REFUGE

IN A CONTEMPORARY TOWN HOUSE

R efinement, elegance, finesse and precision are the fundamental qualities of this urban home, designed by Kurt Neirynck, an interior architect for Obumex. They transform this space from a house into a home.

The office spaces and private lounge provide the best examples of this approach.

P. 82-83

Virtually all of the furniture is fixed. The alcoves, bookcase, desk and desk cupboards have all been made to measure and stained to match the oak floor panels. This light coloured wood was chosen by Obumex.

P. 84-85
The movable furniture pieces are from the Promemoria and Christian Liaigre collections; the customised woods and fabrics create a harmonious ensemble. The rugs were also supplied by Obumex.

AN OASIS

OF PEACE AND RELAXATION

D e Wilde has been producing private indoor and outdoor swimming pools for over thirty years.

This outdoor swimming pool is an oasis of peace and relaxation for many months of the year. The shutter cover and automatic heat control system regulate the temperature of the water, meaning that the pool is always inviting.

The design of swimming pools made from reinforced concrete has improved substantially over the years. Today's designs are guaranteed to be perfectly waterproof and extremely long-lasting. By lining the pool with concrete on site, it is possible to adapt the dimensions and shape to the client's specific requirements.

P. 88-91
The pool is lined with a Bisazza glass mosaic. This luxurious material, when combined with a natural stone surround, lends itself beautifully to any pool, regardless of shape or finish.

RELAXATION AND FITNESS

IN AN AUTHENTIC FAMILY HOME

Interior architect Gilles de Meulemeester has adapted this interior – originally designed over fifteen years ago by the now deceased Jean de Meulder – and created new recreational spaces, a fitness room and a swimming pool in a simple and contemporary style.

P. 92-93
The attic has been converted into a recreational space for entertaining guests and furnished with a bar, pool table and home cinema system.

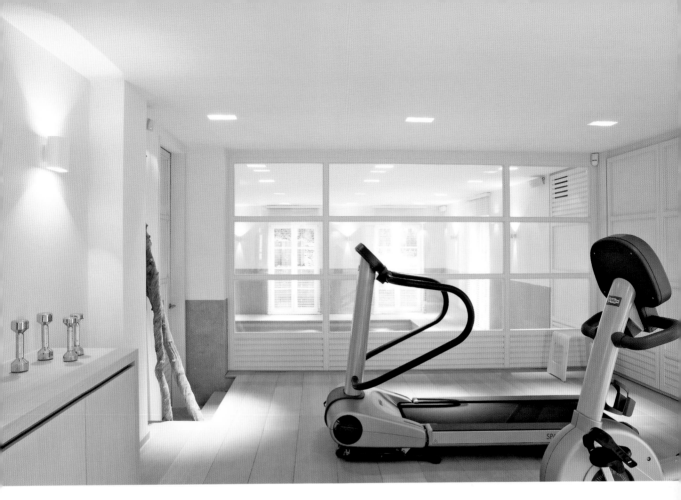

P. 94-97
The fitness room with the indoor pool behind.
The pool deck area is made of a natural grey stone that has been treated with acid.

P. 98-99
The Turkish bath is decorated with a Sicis mosaic.
The walls of the open shower are made from the same grey stone as the swimming pool.

LEISURE SPACES

IN A HISTORIC FINCA

C arrascosa is a historic finca located just outside of Jerez de la Frontera (in the south of Spain) on the edge of an area of unspoilt natural wilderness that extends for more than eighty kilometres along the Bay of Cadiz and reaches almost as far as the Rock of Gibraltar.

Christine Bekaert has transformed the existing buildings (most of which were boarded up) into a beautiful winter haven.

Michel Ceuterick is responsible for the architectural design of the two new wings connected by an imposing tower.

This feature presents the leisure spaces in this exceptional home. The oriental atmosphere that prevails throughout the rooms lends itself perfectly to relaxation.

The walls in this bathroom are partially decorated with hand-made zelliges from Fez. The floor and the bath surround are made of Spanish marble from Gerona. The ceiling was inspired by the traditional hispano-arab steam rooms that can still be found in southern Andalusia.

The antique hand-woven wool rug is from the Aït Ouarain tribe from the Mid-Atlas mountains. The small Mashrabiya table was made to order in a Marrakech souk.

A wenge wood desk. The floor cushions are from the Oussada tribes in the Mid-Atlas.

A varnished wooden Chinese rice jar, a Zemmour rug from the Atlas mountains and some sari cushions from Calcutta create a harmony of red shades. The leather saddle embroidered with silver was found in the imperial city of Meknes.

The walls of this bathroom have been decorated using a combination of artisan zelliges and hand-smoothed tadelakt. The wall lamps and washbasins are made of white copper.

A SERENE ATMOSPHERE

N athalie Van Reeth has transformed this former storeroom into a spa and fitness suite where calmness and serenity abound.

The fitness room has been installed in the original building, while the showers and Turkish bath are housed in the extension, which has been built in the style of a wooden barn. The relaxation area is secluded off by a low wall.

P. 104-107
The simplicity of the design is mirrored in the choice of materials: cement walls, an afzelia wood floor, Moroccan zelliges in the Turkish bath and black painted MDF furniture.

A MONOCHROME PALETTE

FOR A RESTORED FARMHOUSE

This narrow swimming pool (4 x 12 m) has been built in the barn of a restored farmhouse.

The pool was built by Antheunis and is decorated with a beige marble mosaic from Van den Weghe. The floor is made of distressed stippled Cenia marble from Spain.

The beige monochrome walls were created by Couleurs Tadelakt/Odilon Creations.

Only a linen curtain separates the swimming pool area from the bathroom. Under-floor heating has been installed throughout. The window design and curtains are by La Campagne.

P. 110-111
The stippled Cenia marble provides the perfect anti-slip finish. The linen-covered settees are by Cheffertons and the wine table and lamp are by La Campagne.

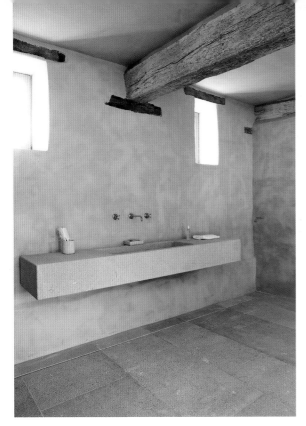

P. 112-113
The bath room: access to the toilets is on the left and the shower is on the right. The towel racks and plumbing fittings are by Volevatch. The washbasin was produced by Van den Weghe. It is made from the same marble as the floor, which extends into the shower. The shower walls have been finished with waterproof tadelakt.

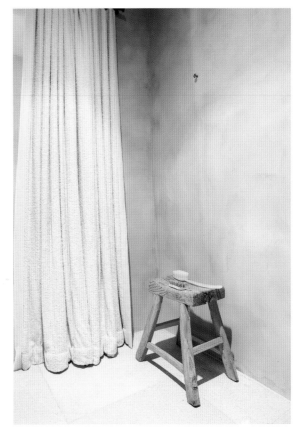

AN AIR OF TRANQUIL LUXURY

 C ustomised designs are one of Obumex's main fortes.

The company has entirely transformed this home in collaboration with the design firm Froment-Delaunois.

The design for this contemporary home is the creation of Xavier Gadeyne, an interior architect for Obumex, who coordinated every aspect of the interior finishings.

P. 114-115
Lounge area with furniture by Promemoria. The small desk was tailor-made by Obumex.

AN UNUSUAL

BEDROOM-CUM-LOUNGE

T he architecture and interior design firm Themenos has beautifully evoked the atmosphere of a luxury suite by incorporating a fireplace and lounge area into the master bedroom of this large country residence.

P. 116-117
Hand-sanded oak panelling is used throughout the bedroom and lounge area of this master suite.
The oak flooring is also hand-sanded.

HOME SERIES

Volume 12 : SPACES FOR LEISURE

The reports in this book are selected from the Beta-Plus collection of home-design books: www.betaplus.com
They have been compiled in a special series by Le Figaro in French language: Ma Déco

PUBLISHER
Beta-Plus Publishing
Termuninck 3
B – 7850 Enghien
Belgium
www.betaplus.com
info@betaplus.com

TEXT
Alexandra Druesne

PHOTOGRAPHY
Jo Pauwels

DESIGN
Polydem - Nathalie Binart

TRANSLATIONS
Txt-Ibis

ISBN : 978-90-8944-043-3

Printed in China

P. 120-121
A table laid by Ingrid Lesage (Finobello) for a small gathering of friends. Lloyd Loom chairs from Vincent Sheppard.

P. 122-123
The swimming pool of a country home created by architect Stéphane Boens.

P. 124-125
A relaxing bedroom-cum-lounge designed by interior designer Helena van den Driessche. Produced by Jos Reynders Décor.

P. 126-127
The teenagers' area in a house that has been re-designed by Philip Simoen.
Tailor-made cupboards by Sphere Concepts.